Antarctica

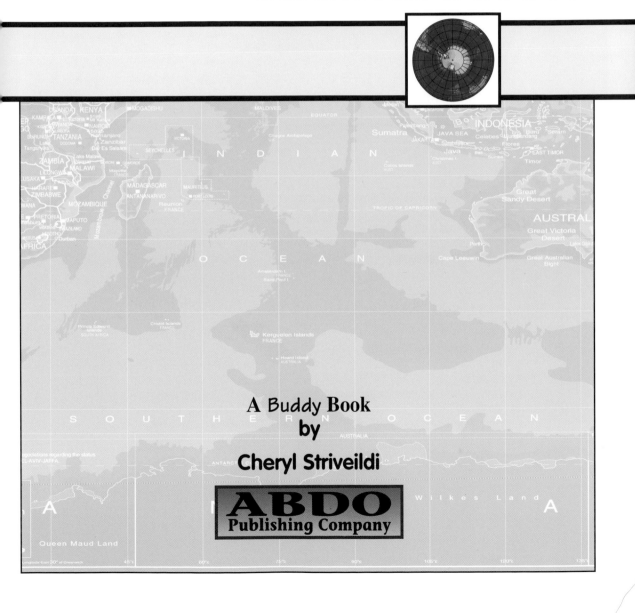

A Buddy Book
by

Cheryl Striveildi

ABDO
Publishing Company

VISIT US AT
www.abdopub.com

Published by Buddy Books, an imprint of ABDO Publishing Company, 4940 Viking Drive, Edina, Minnesota 55435. Copyright © 2003 by Abdo Consulting Group, Inc. International copyrights reserved in all countries. No part of this book may be reproduced in any form without written permission from the publisher.

Printed in the United States.

Edited by: Christy DeVillier
Contributing Editors: Matt Ray, Michael P. Goecke
Graphic Design: M. Hosley
Image Research: Deborah Coldiron
Photographs: Corbis, Corel, Digital Stock, Getty Images, Hulton Archive, Image Ideas Inc., Minden Pictures, Photodisc

Library of Congress Cataloging-in-Publication Data

Striveildi, Cheryl, 1971-
   Continents. Antarctica / Cheryl Striveildi.
      p. cm.
   Includes index.
   Summary: A very brief introduction to the geography, plants, and animals of Antarctica.
   ISBN 1-57765-959-7
      1. Antarctica—Juvenile literature. [1. Antarctica.] I. Title: Antarctica. II. Title.

G863 .S87 2003
919.8'9—dc21

                                        2002074664

Table of Contents

Seven Continents

Water covers most of the earth. Land covers the rest. The earth has seven main land areas, or **continents**. The seven continents are:

 North America   Africa

 South America   Asia

 Europe   Australia

 Antarctica

Antarctica is the coldest continent.

Antarctica is the fifth-largest continent. It covers about 5,100,400 square miles (13,209,000 sq km).

Antarctica is a great wilderness. Scientists go to Antarctica to study it. Some people like to visit Antarctica. But nobody lives there. It is too cold.

Where Is Antarctica?

The earth's bottom half is the Southern Hemisphere. Antarctica is in the Southern Hemisphere. The South Pole is near the center of Antarctica.

Three oceans form a body of water around Antarctica. This body of water is the Southern Ocean. The Southern Ocean is also called the Antarctic Ocean. It is the stormiest ocean on earth.

The closest landmass to Antarctica is South America. It is more than 600 miles (966 km) away.

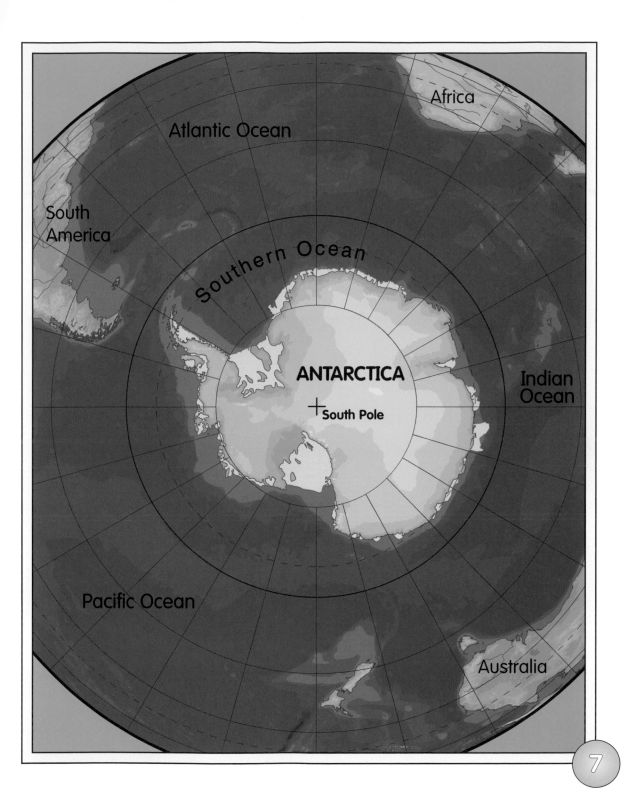

Africa

Atlantic Ocean

South
America

Southern Ocean

ANTARCTICA

+ South Pole

Indian
Ocean

Pacific Ocean

Australia

7

Coldest Place

Antarctica is the coldest place in the world. It is freezing cold most of the time. The coldest area is the middle of the continent. It is warmer along Antarctica's coast.

Antarctica is very windy, too. Blizzards are common there. Blizzards are windy snowstorms. In Antarctica, blizzards can last for days.

In Antarctica, winter lasts from May through September. Winter is a dark time in Antarctica. The sun does not rise for many months.

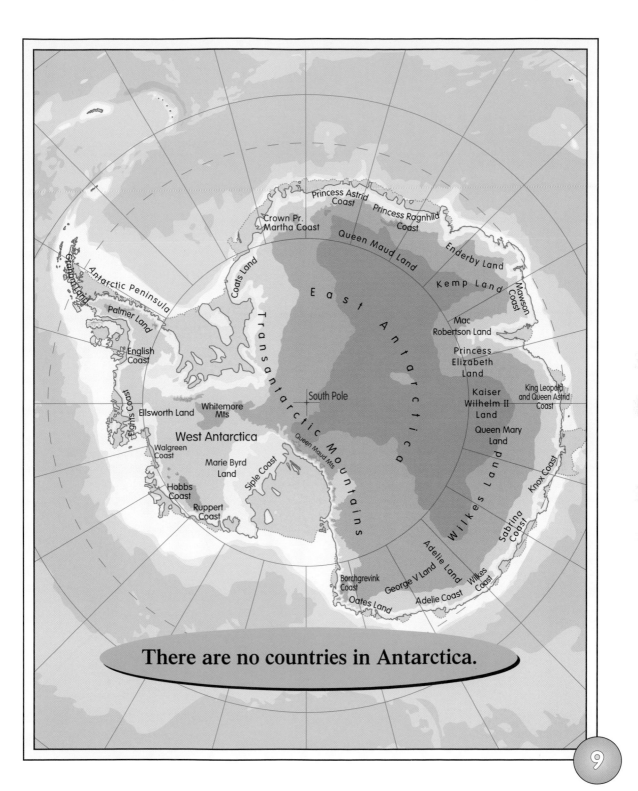

There are no countries in Antarctica.

Land Of Ice

Ice covers most of Antarctica. This ice sheet is the largest body of ice in the world. In some places, the ice is 11,500 feet (3,505 m) thick. That is equal to 10 skyscrapers stacked on top of each other.

An ice sheet covers most of Antarctica.

Ice shelf

Parts of Antarctica's ice sheet float in the water. These parts are called ice shelves. Many of Antarctica's ice shelves have names. The biggest one is the Ross Ice Shelf. It is as big as France.

Pieces of ice often break off the ice shelves. These pieces of ice are called icebergs.

Antarctica has a lot of ice. But it does not have much water. This makes Antarctica the driest place in the world. Some people call Antarctica the Polar Desert.

Icebergs float in the ocean around Antarctica.

Boats sail through icy waters
to reach Antarctica.

Land Of Peace

In 1959, many countries signed the Antarctic Treaty. They agreed not to use Antarctica for war. Many people hope Antarctica will always be a land of peace.

Mining is not allowed in Antarctica, either. Instead, scientists study Antarctica to learn more about the earth.

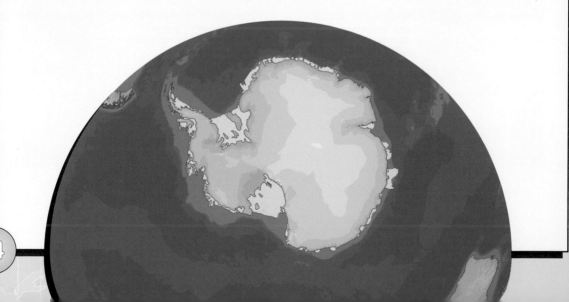

A science station in
Paradise Bay, Antarctica

Plant Life

No trees grow in Antarctica. Only a few places on this continent have plant life.

Two kinds of flowering plants grow in Antarctica. They are hair grass and pearlwort. They grow on Antarctica's northern peninsula.

King penguins in hair grass.

About 80 kinds of mosses grow in Antarctica. Lichens grow there, too. Lichens look like moss. They can be gray, green, yellow, or brown.

Lichens grow in Antarctica.

Lichens have no flowers, leaves, or roots. Many kinds grow on rocks. Some lichens grow less than one inch (three cm) after 100 years. Some lichens can live longer than 2,000 years.

Lichens may be gray, green, yellow, or brown.

Animals

Many kinds of whales swim in the oceans near Antarctica. There are humpback whales, blue whales, and sperm whales. Some whales feed on krill. Krill are tiny animals that look like shrimp.

Humpback whales feeding on krill.

Krill

Humpback whale

A blue whale blowing spray

Tail of a sperm whale

Penguins live in Antarctica, too. Penguins are birds that cannot fly. But they swim very well. Penguins have fat that keeps them warm. Their special down feathers help, too.

Adélie penguins

Many kinds of penguins live in Antarctica. There are Adélie penguins, macaroni penguins, king penguins, and chinstrap penguins. The largest kind is the emperor penguin. Adult emperor penguins weigh about 65 pounds (29 kg).

Emperor penguin

Chinstrap penguin

Adélie penguins

Macaroni penguins

23

Leopard seal

Seals are Antarctic animals, too. They mostly live in the water. The biggest seals in the world are elephant seals. They can grow to become 16 feet (5 m) long.

Most seals eat fish, krill, or squid. Leopard seals hunt other seals, too.

Young fur seals

Elephant seals

Roald Amundsen

Roald Amundsen was the first person to reach the South Pole. He was an explorer from Norway. He reached the pole on December 14, 1911.

Roald Amundsen (right) at the South Pole in 1911.

Visiting Antarctica

The best time to visit Antarctica is in December and January. These are summer months in Antarctica. On some summer days, the sun does not go down.

Daylight can last for 24 hours in Antarctica.

There are many beautiful sights in Antarctica.

People can fly or sail to Antarctica. Visitors can ski, climb mountains, and camp in Antarctica. They often visit the science stations there. Many people agree that Antarctica is a beautiful place.

Sightseeing from a helicopter.

Antarctica

- Antarctica is the fifth-largest continent.

- Antarctica is the coldest place in the world.

- Antarctica is the driest continent.

- No trees grow in Antarctica.

- Antarctica's highest point is the top of Mount Vinson Massif.

- Antarctica's biggest ice shelf is the Ross Ice Shelf.

Important Words

continent one of the earth's seven main land areas.

hemisphere one half of the earth.

ice shelf the part of Antarctica's ice sheet that floats in the ocean.

iceberg a big chunk of ice floating in water.

lichens plants without flowers, leaves, and roots.

mining digging into the earth for coal or other minerals.

peninsula a long piece of land that juts into the sea. A peninsula is joined to a bigger landmass.

Web Sites

Would you like to learn more about Antarctica?
Please visit ABDO Publishing Company on the World Wide Web to find web site links about Antarctica. These links are routinely monitored and updated to provide the most current information available.

www.abdopub.com

Index